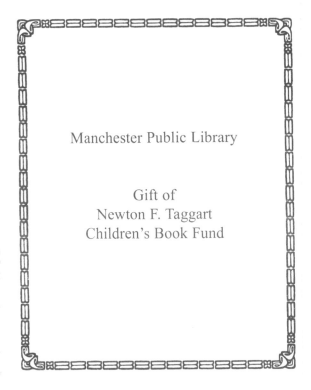

A Robbie Reader

DEREK CARR

Mitchell Lane
PUBLISHERS
2001 SW 31st Avenue
Hallandale, FL 33009
www.mitchelllane.com

Tammy
Gagne

Mitchell Lane
PUBLISHERS

Printing   1   2   3   4   5   6   7   8   9

A Robbie Reader Biography

Aaron Rodgers	Derek Carr	Meghan Markle
Abigail Breslin	Derrick Rose	Mia Hamm
Adam Levine	Donovan McNabb	Michael Strahan
Adrian Peterson	Drake Bell & Josh Peck	Miguel Cabrera
Albert Einstein	Dr. Seuss	Miley Cyrus
Albert Pujols	Dustin Pedroia	Miranda Cosgrove
Aly and AJ	Dwayne Johnson	Philo Farnsworth
Andrew Luck	Dwyane Wade	Prince Harry
AnnaSophia Robb	Dylan & Cole Sprouse	Raven-Symoné
Ariana Grande	Ed Sheeran	Rixton
Ashley Tisdale	Emily Osment	Robert Griffin III
Brenda Song	Ezekiel Elliott	Roy Halladay
Brittany Murphy	Hailee Steinfeld	Shaquille O'Neal
Bruno Mars	Harry Styles	Shawn Mendes
Buster Posey	Hilary Duff	Story of Harley-Davidson
Carmelo Anthony	Jamie Lynn Spears	Sue Bird
Charles Schulz	Jennette McCurdy	Syd Hoff
Chris Johnson	Jeremy Lin	Tiki Barber
Clayton Kershaw	Jesse McCartney	Tim Howard
Cliff Lee	Jimmie Johnson	Tim Lincecum
Colin Kaepernick	Joe Flacco	Tom Brady
Dak Prescott	Johnny Gruelle	Tony Hawk
Dale Earnhardt Jr.	Jonas Brothers	Troy Polamalu
Darius Rucker	Keke Palmer	Tyler Perry
David Archuleta	Kristaps Porzingis	Victor Cruz
Debby Ryan	Larry Fitzgerald	Victoria Justice
Demi Lovato	LeBron James	

Library of Congress Cataloging-in-Publication Data
Names: Gagne, Tammy author.
Title: Derek Carr / by Tammy Gagne.
Description: Hallandale, Florida : Mitchell Lane Publishers, [2019] | Series: A Robbie Reader | Includes bibliographical references and index. | Audience: Ages: 5-9.
Identifiers: LCCN 2018008724| ISBN 9781680201901 (library bound)
Subjects: LCSH: Carr, Derek, 1991- —Juvenile literature. | Quarterbacks (Football)—United States—Biography—Juvenile literature. | Oakland Raiders (Football team)—History—Juvenile literature.
Classification: LCC GV939.C3746 G35 2018 | DDC 796.332092 [B] —dc23
LC record available at https://lccn.loc.gov/2018008724

eBook ISBN: 978-1-68020-191-8

ABOUT THE AUTHOR: Tammy Gagne has written more than 200 books for both adults and children. Her titles include numerous books about athletes—including *Kristaps Porzingis* and *Calvin Johnson*. She resides in northern New England with her husband and son.

PUBLISHER'S NOTE: The following story has been thoroughly researched and to the best of our knowledge represents a true story. While every possible effort has been made to ensure accuracy, the publisher will not assume liability for damages caused by inaccuracies in the data, and makes no warranty on the accuracy of the information contained herein. This story has not been authorized or endorsed by Derek Carr.

CONTENTS

Words in bold type can be found in the glossary.

Oakland Raiders quarterback Derek Carr threw 103 touchdown passes in his first four seasons in the NFL.

1 DEREK'S $125 MILLION DEAL

"**I**'ve got one," Dad announced as he sat down for dinner with family. Who wrote the novel *Robinson Crusoe*?" The Davis family played a little game each evening while they ate. One person tossed out a trivia question, and the first one to answer it correctly could ask another. Garrett and his sister, Paige, always said the game was boring. But their enthusiasm said otherwise.

"Oooh, I know!" Garrett said. "Daniel Defoe, right?" He loved beating Paige to questions about books. Two years older, she had read many more of them than Garrett had. The only place where he could stump

> **The Davis family played a little game each evening while they ate.**

her sometimes was sports—and still only sometimes.

> Garrett's mind wandered back to Derek Carr. He had been Garrett's favorite quarterback long before he became one of the highest-paid players.

"That's correct," Dad answered. "Your turn, kiddo."

Garrett wanted to stump his sister. Then he remembered something he heard on the radio that morning. "Which Oakland Raiders player just signed a contract for $125 million?"

"That's easy," Paige declared. "Derek Carr." She didn't even ask if she was right.

"That's a lot of money," Dad said. "Do you think he is worth all that?"

"Actually," Garrett replied, "Carr himself said he doesn't think he deserves it. But his teammates all said that they think he does. They all told the press how hard he works for the team."

"Interesting," Dad said. "It sounds like he is a **humble** young man. Now, Paige, I believe it's your turn." Garrett smiled. No one ever really won the trivia game. They just kept playing. But it truly was a fun way to pass the time while they ate.

As Paige was thinking of the next question, Garrett's mind wandered back to Derek Carr. He had been Garrett's favorite quarterback long before he became one of the highest-paid players. Even though he had only been playing in the NFL since 2014, Derek had already shown himself to be one of its most talented and dedicated athletes.

2 A FOOTBALL FAMILY

Derek Dallas Carr was born in Fresno, California, on March 28, 1991. The youngest child of Rodger and Sheryl Carr, Derek had two older brothers, David and Darren. All three boys grew up going to church and playing football. Derek's grandfather was the pastor at Liberty Christian Center in Bakersfield. David would go on to play quarterback in the NFL, initially for the Houston Texans. Darren would become a high school football coach after playing on defense at the college level.

Derek was still a preteen when David was **drafted** first overall by Houston in 2002. The family moved to Texas to be near

Derek initially played high school football for Clements High School in Sugar Land.

him as he started his pro career. Being so close to a professional football team gave Derek the chance to learn even more about the sport. His father remembers how Derek would go to David's games and know what David should and would do next on the field. He had an understanding of the game far beyond that of other kids his age.

Derek initially played high school football for Clements High School in Sugar Land. In his sophomore and junior seasons, he passed for 2,868 yards and 28 touchdowns. After the family moved back to California, Derek spent his senior year playing for Bakersfield Christian High School. That season he threw for an astounding

David Carr

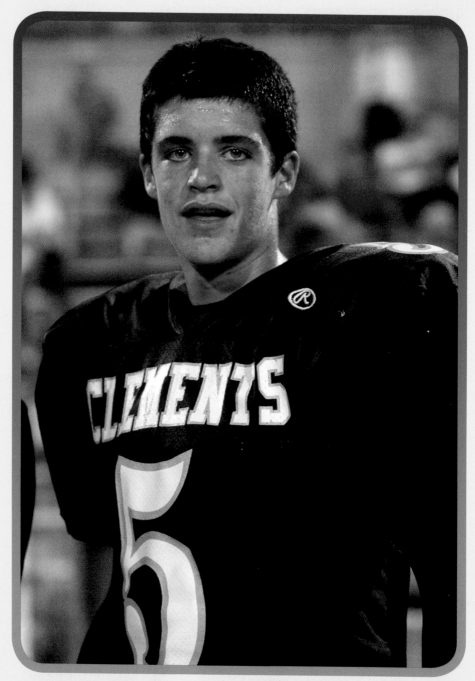

Derek starred at quarterback for Clements High School and then Bakersfield Christian High School. As a senior, he threw for 544 yards in one game.

4,067 yards and 46 touchdowns. By the time he graduated in 2009, several universities with prestigious football programs wanted Derek to enroll. But Derek wanted to go to Fresno State. In addition to being David's **alma mater**, the school was known for producing successful quarterbacks. Trent Dilfer, Kevin Sweeney,

Derek followed in his older brother's footsteps. Both David (left) and Derek (right) achieved greatness as quarterbacks for Fresno State.

> Derek's family had brought him up to be a responsible person. But when he went to college, he began acting out.

and Billy Volek all attended Fresno State.

Derek's family had brought him up to be a responsible person. But when he went to college, he began acting out. Instead of focusing on his studies and football, Derek was spending most of his time going to parties. If he had continued down that path, he might never have made it to the NFL. In 2013, Derek told *The New York Times*, "I was out running around, living the life. Everyone wanted to hang out with the Next Big Thing, and I soaked it up like an idiot. I want to go back and punch that guy in the face."

Fresno State Bulldogs

3 GETTING BACK ON TRACK

Shortly after Derek entered Fresno State, he met a fellow student named Heather Neel at BJ's Restaurant and Brewhouse. Heather was working as a waitress at the restaurant while she pursued her teaching degree. She and Derek soon discovered that they had a lot in common and started dating. But when Heather realized how much he was partying, she wrote Derek a letter. In it she told him how disappointed she was by his behavior. The person he was acting like wasn't at all the person she had thought he was.

> She and Derek soon discovered that they had a lot in common and started dating.

Derek and his wife, Heather, attend the 52nd Academy of Country Music Awards in 2017.

Derek has said that letter changed his life. He got back on track and ended up performing better than any other quarterback in Fresno State's history. During his career with the Bulldogs, he racked up 12,842 passing yards and 113 touchdown passes. He was also the top college player in the country during his senior year in five different categories, including passing yards (5,082) and passing touchdowns (50).

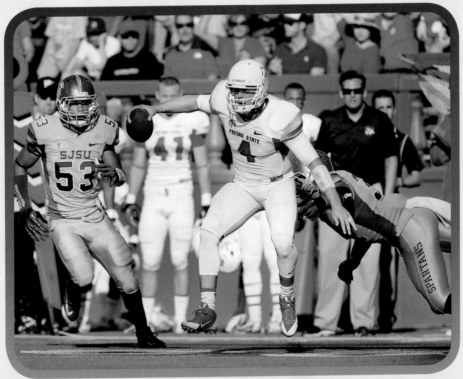

Derek has a powerful arm, but he can also pick up first downs with his feet, as he does here during a game against San Jose State in 2013.

Derek and Heather married on June 29, 2012. The following summer, Heather gave birth to the couple's first child. They named him Dallas, Derek's middle name. The letter D is mighty popular in the Carr family.

> Derek and Heather said that watching their son go through the life-threatening situation was extremely difficult.

David's middle name is Duke while Darren's middle is Douglas. In Derek's case, his middle name came from two places. Dallas was the name of a favorite coach Rodger had in school. Sheryl was also born near the city of Dallas–in Waxahachie, Texas.

When Derek and Heather's son was born, he suffered from a dangerous medical condition. It caused the baby's **intestines** to tangle together in knots. Fortunately, doctors were able to correct the problem with surgery. Still, Derek and Heather said that watching their son go through the life-threatening situation was extremely difficult.

Derek spends a little time in the end zone with his son, Dallas, before the start of a Fresno State game in 2014.

The following year was better for Derek in more ways than one. First and foremost, his son was healthy again. Then in the 2014 NFL Draft, the Oakland Raiders chose Derek as their second-round pick. All his hard work was about to pay off. He was about to become a professional football player.

Derek's dream of playing in the NFL became a reality when the Oakland Raiders drafted him in 2014. Here he takes part in drills during the Oakland Raiders Rookie Minicamp that year.

4 LEADING HIS TEAM

Derek kept working hard as he joined his new teammates. This dedication combined with his ability earned him a starting position on the field. The rookie quarterback threw his first touchdown pass during his first game. With just under three minutes left in the first quarter, he fired the ball to wide receiver Rod Streater, who then took it straight into the end zone.

Derek quickly became known for his arm strength. In a game against the Kansas City Chiefs, he fired a 25-yard pass to Michael Crabtree. With opposing players on either side of him, Crabtree caught the pass just

> The rookie quarterback threw his first touchdown pass during his first game.

over the goal line as the crowd cheered. The announcers and the audience alike marveled at how flawlessly the quarterback and wide receiver had worked together to score for their team.

Derek led Oakland to a 12-4 season in 2016. Here, in a game against the Kansas City Chiefs, Derek runs with the ball while being pursued by Chiefs linebacker Frank Zombo.

During his first three years in the NFL, Derek continued to perform well on the field. His numbers matched those of some of the greatest quarterbacks in history. Although some people questioned whether

In 2016, Derek broke his leg during the fourth quarter of a game against the Indianapolis Colts. The injury, which required surgery, took him off the field for the rest of the season.

he was worthy of the $125 million contract the Raiders offered him in 2017, many fans think he has the potential to be one of the top NFL quarterbacks.

The 2016 season was a challenging one for Derek. In a game against the Indianapolis Colts, Derek broke his **fibula**. The leg injury took him off the field for the rest of the season. The Raiders finished 12-4 that year. But without their star quarterback, they lost in the first round of the playoffs. But Derek came back strong in 2017. He was named to the **Pro Bowl** for the third straight season.

> The 2016 season was a challenging one for Derek.

Kevin Byard of the Tennessee Titans celebrates with Derek during the NFL Pro Bowl between the AFC and NFC on January 28, 2018.

5 FAITH, FAMILY, AND FOOTBALL

In 2016, Derek and Heather welcomed their second son, Deker. Derek has said that the other things more important to him than football are his faith and his family. He thinks that they become even more important as he becomes more successful in football. He wants to give his best to all three of these parts of his life.

When Derek isn't on the football field or with his family, he is helping others. One of the things he enjoys most is preaching like his grandfather. Sometimes when he goes home to Bakersfield, he speaks at the church services.

> Derek has said that the other things more important to him than football are his faith and his family.

Derek's faith is a big part of his life. He is seen here leading his team-mates and players from the Houston Texans in prayer after a game in Mexico City, Mexico.

Derek also donates his time to Valley Children's Hospital, where doctors saved his son's life back in 2013. In addition to appearing in ads for the hospital, Derek also spends time with the young patients. He has taken part in tea parties and go-kart races with kids who

When Derek isn't on the football field or with his family, he is helping others.

are fighting diseases such as **cystic fibrosis** and **lymphoma** during his visits. Derek has said that seeing smiles on the kids' faces is amazing.

Derek enjoys meeting his many fans. He always tries to make time to sign autographs for them.

Derek hopes to have a long career in the NFL. But he has a few ideas about what he will do when his playing days are behind him. He told the *Fresno Bee*, "I'm going to keep preaching. I don't know if I'll have a church or [be] preaching different places but it's definitely what I'm going to be doing. Maybe I'll coach, who knows? Maybe at Fresno one day. Who knows? I will never close a door on anything."

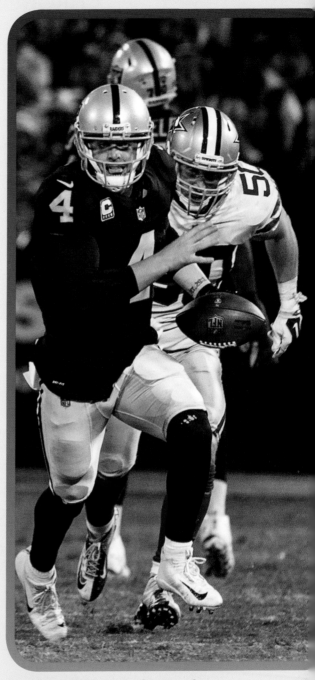

Derek is still showing his worth on the field, as in this game against the Dallas Cowboys.

CHRONOLOGY

1991 Derek Dallas Carr is born on March 28.

2009 Derek graduates from Bakersfield Christian High School. He enters Fresno State and begins playing for the Bulldogs.

2012 Derek marries Heather Neel.

2013 Derek and Heather's first son, Dallas, is born.

2014 The Oakland Raiders select Derek with their second-round draft pick.

2015 Derek makes the Pro Bowl for the first time.

2016 Derek and Heather's second son, Deker, is born. After breaking his leg during a game, Derek is out for the rest of the season.

2017 The Raiders sign Derek to a $125 million contract.

CAREER STATS

Year	Team	PA	PC	Y	TD
2011	Fresno State	446	279	3,544	26
2012	Fresno State	511	344	4,104	37
2013	Fresno State	659	454	5,083	50
2014	Oakland Raiders	599	348	3,270	21
2015	Oakland Raiders	573	350	3,987	32
2016	Oakland Raiders	560	357	3,937	28
2017	Oakland Raiders	515	323	3,496	22

PA = passes attempted, PC = passes completed, Y = yardage, TD = touchdowns

FIND OUT MORE

ESPN. Derek Carr. http://www.espn.com/nfl/player/_/
id/16757/derek-carr

Fishman, Jon M. *Derek Carr*. Minneapolis, MN: Lerner,
2018.

Morey, Allan. *The Oakland Raiders Story*. Minneapolis,
MN: Bellwether Media, 2017.

NFL website. https://www.nfl.com/

Oakland Raiders website. http://www.raiders.com/

Scheff, Matt. *Derek Carr*. Mendota Heights, MN: Focus
Readers, 2018.

WORKS CONSULTED

Badenhausen, Kurt. "The NFL's Highest-Paid Players
2017." *Forbes*, September 18, 2017. https://www.
forbes.com/sites/kurtbadenhausen/2017/09/18/
the-nfls-highest-paid-players-2017/#5fd36b8d130e

Dubin, Jared. "Derek Carr on his record-breaking $125M
extension: 'I don't feel like I deserve it.'" CBS Sports,
June 24, 2017. https://www.cbssports.com/nfl/
news/derek-carr-on-his-record-breaking-125m-
extension-i-dont-feel-like-i-deserve-it/

Galaviz, Anthony. "Raiders' Derek Carr might have
missed out on success if not for wife's intervention."
The Fresno Bee, August 27, 2017. http://www.
fresnobee.com/sports/nfl/article169567077.html

Galaviz, Anthony. "What? Derek Carr's first love was
basketball? Here are more surprises about Raiders
QB." *The Fresno Bee*, July 21, 2017. http://www.
fresnobee.com/sports/nfl/article162893673.html

WORKS CONSULTED

Jacobs, Melissa. "Derek Carr's broken leg spells certain end to Raiders' Super Bowl hopes." December 25, 2016. https://www.si.com/nfl/2016/12/25/derek-carr-raiders-broken-leg

LeBaron, Dan. "How Derek Carr's first three seasons stack up against the league's elite quarterbacks." SB Nation, June 23, 2017. https://www.silverandblackpride.com/2017/6/23/15864202/how-derek-carrs-first-three-seasons-stack-up-against-the-leagues-elite-quarterbacks

LeBlanc, Nick. "Derek Carr displays faith, leadership." The Feather Online, April 14, 2016. https://www.thefeather.com/2016/04/14/derek-carr-shares-journey-towards-chasing-nfl-dream/

Lipton, Ryan. "Look: Raiders' Derek Carr's best accomplishments in first 3 seasons." *USA Today*, June 24, 2017. http://raiderswire.usatoday.com/2017/06/24/look-raiders-derek-carrs-best-accomplishments-in-first-3-seasons/

Paskal, Eddie. "Derek Carr's Top 10 Moments As A Raider So Far." Raiders.com, March 28, 2016. http://www.raiders.com/news/article-1/Derek-Carrs-Top-10-Moments-As-A-Raider-So-Far/322993bb-957f-41e6-9ffa-e80613b9363a

Syed, Razi. "Raiders' Derek Carr spends time with patients at Valley Children's." *The Fresno Bee*, May 13, 2016. http://www.fresnobee.com/sports/article77717412.html

WORKS CONSULTED

White, David. "Harrowing Moments Far From the Field." *The New York Times*, August 28, 2013. http://www.nytimes.com/2013/08/29/sports/ncaafootball/at-start-of-preseason-fresno-state-quarterback-faced-a-harrowing-test.html

GLOSSARY

alma mater (AHL-muh MAH-ter)–a school where a person has studied in the past

drafted (DRAHFTED)–selected for a position on a sports team

cystic fibrosis (SIS-tik fi-BROH-sis)–a chronic lung disease that affects young people

fibula (FIB-yuh-luh)–the outer and thinner bone in the human leg

humble (HUHM-buhl)–not arrogant

intestine (in-TES-tin)–a long tubular organ that is part of the digestive system

lymphoma (lim-FOH-muh)–a tumor that grows within a person's lymph nodes

Pro Bowl (PRO BOHL)–the NFL's all-star game

INDEX